Photographic Memory Mastery:

Learn Powerful Techniques to Boost your Memory Instantly & Remember Important Details for Achieving Academic, Work and Business Success

Steve Chambers

© **Copyright 2018 by Steve Chambers - All rights reserved.**

The contents of this book may not be reproduced, duplicated or transmitted without direct written permission from the author.

Under no circumstances will any legal responsibility or blame be held against the publisher for any reparation, damages, or monetary loss due to the information herein, either directly or indirectly.

Legal Notice:

This book is copyright protected. This is only for personal use. You cannot amend, distribute, sell, use, quote or paraphrase any part or the content within this book without the consent of the author.

Disclaimer Notice:

Please note the information contained

within this document is for educational and entertainment purposes only. Every attempt has been made to provide accurate, up to date and reliable complete information. No warranties of any kind are expressed or implied. Readers acknowledge that the author is not engaging in the rendering of legal, financial, medical or professional advice. The content of this book has been derived from various sources. Please consult a licensed professional before attempting any techniques outlined in this book.

By reading this document, the reader agrees that under no circumstances are is the author responsible for any losses, direct or indirect, which are incurred as a result of the use of information contained within this document, including, but not limited to, —errors, omissions, or inaccuracies.

Table of Contents

Introduction

Chapter 1: Photographic Memory Mastery: Getting Started

Chapter 2: How Photographic Memory Works

Chapter 3: Powerful Photographic Memory Techniques Explained

Chapter 4: How to Achieve Photographic Memory

Chapter 5: The Importance of Visualization

Chapter 6: Can My Emotions Make a Difference?

Chapter 7: How to Remember People's Names

Chapter 8: The Steps You Need to Memorize Numbers

Chapter 9: It's All in the Details

Chapter 10: Putting it Altogether – How to Achieve Photographic Memory Mastery

Bonus Chapter: How to Developer Laser Sharp Focus for Better Results

Conclusion

What This Book Will Teach You

Are you curious to learn about Photographic Memory but unsure where to start?

Have you always wanted to remember people's names or numbers better, but end up forgetting these important details?

If these questions relate well with you, then this book is for you. In this book you will find the basic essentials to learning Photographic Memory. This book introduces readers to Photographic Memory, the in's and out, the various processes and steps involved.

Who this Book is for

This book contains information on how to learn Photographic Memory from a beginner level.

Readers who can benefit the most from the book include:

- Students who would like to know more about the Photographic Memory as a skill to use in their studies and helping them remember better to produce better grades and higher scores on their exams.

- Working professionals interested in learning Photographic Memory to help boost their memory for career advancement.

- Entrepreneurs who want to learn Photographic Memory as another important skill to succeed on their business.

How this Book is Organized

This book is organized into three parts.

The parts are best read in chronological order. Once you become familiar with all the steps outlined in the book, you can go directly to the techniques which apply to your current situation the best.

The three parts of the book are:

Part One outlines the essential topics on Photographic Memory, and then how the memory works. The section also talks about how important it is to learn these topics in order to form a solid foundation in doing the right steps – from introductory concepts to applying the powerful techniques in developing a Photographic Memory.

Part Two is about Photographic Memory in more detail. You'll learn how to use visualization and emotions to your advantage as well as techniques on how to remember people's names and numbers.

Part Three is about tying it altogether on gaining Photographic Memory Mastery. Plus, a BONUS Chapter on how to achieve laser sharp focus for better results on memory retention and remembering important information.

Introduction:

Congratulations on owning *Photographic Memory Mastery* and thank you for doing so.

The following chapters will discuss what you need to know to work on your photographic memory and never forget important details again. Many people find themselves wishing for a better memory. They are tired of running into people they have already met and looking silly because they can't remember names. They are tired of being late for work because they can't find the car keys. They are tired of running to the grocery store and then getting home to find they forget something important.

This guidebook will be able to help you fix these issues and more. It will help you to work on your photographic memory so that you are finally able to remember the little details in your life. Anyone can work on their photographic memory, and this guidebook will provide you with the methods and techniques that you need. From learning how the brain stores memories to looking at some simple techniques that will make it easier to remember names and even long strings of numbers, you will soon be able to remember any detail you want.

When you are ready to work on your photographic memory and see the results when it comes to how well you can remember things, make sure to take a look at this guidebook to get started.

There are plenty of books on this subject on the market, thanks again for choosing this one! Every effort was made to ensure it is full of as much useful information as possible, please enjoy!

Chapter 1: Photographic Memory Mastery: Getting Started

Chapter 1: An Overview of a Photographic Memory

1.1

The term photographic memory is something that is becoming ever more popular in our culture today. Just listening to the name itself makes it seem like such a great capability to possess. While we all wonder what it would be like to have this kind of memory and wish that we could have it for ourselves, it is very rare that someone would actually know what this kind of memory truly is. There are plenty of ideas out there about this kind of memory, but to make sure that you really understand what a photographic memory is, you must first dive into some of the science behind this phenomenon.

To start, photographic memory is going to refer to the ability to recall experiences in a lot of details. This happens not only right after the incident occurs, but also a long time after the event occurred. The situation doesn't even have to take that much time out of your life; you would still be able to go through it in details. This is not just a major life event. It may include remembering all the test questions you took five years ago or being able to recite a page of a book with only a few minutes to look at it.

It's important to realize that referring to this ability as only photographic memory isn't always accurate. As we go through and study photographic memory more, you can sometimes hear that it is used interchangeably with an eidetic memory. This isn't completely wrong, but there are some differences between the two that are very important.

When we talk about eidetic memory, it is

the ability to recall experiences and situations in a lot of detail, either shortly after the incident occurs or even months afterward. This may sound like photographic memory, but with an eidetic memory, people are able to recall the situation in their minds as though they were viewing a picture. Then, they are able to use that memory and verbalize the details with extreme accuracy.

When we talk about photographic memory, we are looking at something a bit different. With the most basic definition of this, you will find that photographic memory allows you to recall numbers and words. People who have developed this skill well are able to read length poems and then repeat them word for word, without having to use the page as a guide. They are also able to glance down at a series of numbers for a short amount of time and then be able to recall those numbers, going in the right order, when they are asked.

While there is some distinction between these two types of memory, it is common for people to just use photographic memory and use it as a blanket statement to help cover all the different types of developed memorization abilities.

There are some differences though. With eidetic memory, you will recall the situation like a photograph, and the brain will pick and choose what parts of that picture it wants to focus on. With this type of memory, you may be able to recall a stranger you met in the store and take the time to describe what they wore, their hair color, their weight, and how tall they were. But with a photographic memory, you will remember more of the verbal aspects of the situation. You would be more likely to remember what you discussed with the stranger or what the stranger's name was.

When it comes to the debate about memory, you will find that some doctors and scientists will argue. Their argument brings up two sides of the photographic memory development. Some claim that there are individuals who are born with the photographic memory, and they will be able to recall things in great details when they were only a few months old.

Then, there are those who argue that it is not possible for someone to be born with a photographic memory. They argue that everyone can have this kind of memory, but that some are more in tune with the process, and so they were able to use it more readily than others. It is the same idea that no one was born knowing how to play the piano. But, musicians like Mozart and Beethoven, who were the most advanced geniuses in music to live, were able to hone in on the skill and become great, but only after they first learned how to play the piano.

Some scientists state that these same rules apply when it comes to photographic memory. They think that some children are born with a greater ability to get photographic memory and to sharpen their skills. This doesn't mean that others can't work at it as well. They may just need to take some time to develop their skills first.

This is good news for you if you are looking to gain more of photographic memory. It may not have come naturally to you when you were younger, but it is a skill that you can work on and get better at over time. You just need to take some time to go through the process and train your brain a little bit.

You need to realize that it may take you a bit more time than others, and the process can be slower. Some people do struggle with this kind of memory. But this is possible with almost anything that you work on. You just need to find the techniques that work the best for you, practice daily so that you can properly train your brain, and keep trying. If you are able to keep going with those three simple steps, you will find that it will not take long to develop your own photographic memory.

Eidetic memory and photographic memory are often used interchangeably. There are some differences between the two, but there are also a lot of similarities that show up between them too. Mixing them together is not such a big deal, and we are going to refer to all types of advanced memorization skills in this book under photographic memory to help keep them all in order.

1.2

If you are reading this guidebook, you most likely already have some interest in gaining a photographic memory, and you may already know some of the benefits that come with it. There are actually quite a few benefits of this kind of memory, which makes it something that almost everyone can try out. You may want to pick out a few of the benefits to focus on to use as motivation if the techniques get hard or the training doesn't always go the way that you want. This can help to keep you on track so that you see results. Some of the advantages of having a photographic memory include:

- It allows you to remember even the simplest details that can get lost in the day, which saves you effort and time. With a photographic memory, you will not have to worry about walking into a room and then forgetting what you went in there for. You won't lose your keys and be late for work. You won't miss payments and have to pay late fees on any of your bills again. It can save you so much time and effort, even on some of the simple daily tasks that you need to focus on.

- It helps you to relax when you do some activities because you already know that you are finishing what you need. A good example of this is going to the grocery store. It can be frustrating to head to the store, fight with the crowds to get your stuff and check out, and then get home and find that you forget something that was important.

With a photographic memory, you can complete the task, knowing that you will always remember everything that you need. You will easily get home and have all the items on your list without all the worry.

- It can save you some embarrassment because you will remember the faces and names of those you meet. Without a photographic memory, it is easy to worry about whether you will be able to remember them later on. How often do you run into someone and then don't recognize them, even if the two of you met before. This can make for an embarrassing situation. But with the help of a photographic memory, you can feel better knowing that you will remember that person next time. You will remember their interests, their name, what you discussed before, and even some other details about when you met up the last time.

- It can open up options for your career. Many of the fields that do well could use someone who has a photographic memory. It doesn't matter if you want to do something like law enforcement or the military or even be a teacher, this kind of memory can be helpful. Accounting, banking and more can use it as well. You can open up a lot of doors when you decide to work on your photographic memory, and you will be amazed at how much this can help.

- You can keep memories alive for a long time. Everyone has some memories that are important to them and that they would like to keep around. With a regular memory, parts of those memories are going to start fading, and you will forget some of the details that made those memories so important. With the help of a photographic memory, you can remember all these events, including the details of those events, for a long time to come.
- It is a good tool when preparing for a variety of fields. Whether you are prepping for a test in college, or you are a professional who is preparing for an interview,

having a photographic memory is going to help you remember the details that are needed so that you can succeed. You won't have to spend hours studying or trying to remember facts. The photographic memory will save you a lot of time and hassle so that you can get things done.

Now that you know a little bit more about photographic memory and what it means, especially compared to some other forms of memory recollection, it is time to move on and learn how to get started with improving your own!

1.3

Now that we know a little bit more about

photographic memory, it is time to look at some of the steps that you should be able to follow in order to get started. the steps here are basic since we havne't really looked at the techniques that are needed for this skill. The steps you can do include:

1. Come up with your reason why for enhancing your photographic memory

2. Get in the right frame of mind to help you start.

3. Understand that everyone learns at a different pace. You may not learn as fast as others, but you will get there.

4. Set aside some time each day, at least an hour, to progress through the techniques we will discuss.

Your Quick Start Action Step:

The quick start action step for this chapter is to think through the reasons why you want to learn how to enhance your photographic memory. Everyone has a different reason, but yours will be your motivation through the rest of the steps. Write it down and keep it someplace you can look over any time you need that little push.

Chapter 2: How Photographic Memory Works

Chapter 2:
Undesrstanding Memory

2.1

Memory is a very important part of how the brain works. It is the ability of your mind to retain and then later retrieve information that is important. To better understand how the brain is able to process information to make it into a memory; you must know the three main stages of memory creation. These are encoding, storage, and retrieval.

Encoding is the part that will happen when the brain registers some kind of stimulus that the body receives through the senses. The stimulus can be pretty much anything, as long as it triggers the body to respond or react in some way. Attention can pay a big role in this process because it helps to determine whether the brain will encode the information or not. The more attention you give to a particular stimulus, the more likely it will be encoded.

The next step is the storage phase, and it's the process of retention. This is where the brain will need to filter through the information and put it either in short-term memory or long-term memory. There are different things that will determine where a memory will end up, but emotions tend to have a big impact on this as well. Those memories that have a lot of emotions tied to them are more likely to be stored in the long-term memory.

And then there is the retrieval stage. This is the process where the mind will look for and recall the information that is already stored. This is when the memory is actually a memory because this stage is where we are going to do our "remembering."

One of the models that have helped to influence the study of memory is known as the Atkinson-Shiffrin memory mode. This was a model that was proposed by Richard Atkinson, a professional of psychology, and Richard Shiffrin, a professional of cognitive science in 1968. With this model, the human memory is composed of three main components. These components include a sensory register, the long-term memory, and the short-term memory.

2.2

Understanding how the memory works can be so important when it comes to helping you remember things. If you don't learn how these parts all work, it becomes really hard for you to put any information into the long-term memory. Short-term memory is going to only hold onto things for a few minutes, but not much longer. If that is only as long as you can hold onto information, you will never have a photographic memory. Learning how to put things into the long-term memory will make all the difference and can help make the whole process easier.

2.3

Memory is stored in several different places. Whether it is found in the short-term or the long term, memory will make a difference on whether you are able to remember it or not. Let's look at some of the different parts of the memory to see how they work together.

1. **Sensory register**

The sensory register is the stimulus that is received through one or more of the senses. This one may not even reach the storage phase and can be neglected or forgotten. There are a ton of stimuli that reach us each day and the brain is designed to ignore most of these because it would end up overwhelming us to take it all in. This means that most of the stimuli that we encounter through the day will be ignored and we will never even think about it. But if we give one of the stimuli enough attention, then it has the potential to be stored inside the short-term memory.

2. Short-term memory

The short-term memory is often known to as the working memory. This is any memory that will stay in the brain for about 18 to 30 seconds. If you do not rehearse the information and let the brain know that the information is important, then it is likely going to disappear, and you won't remember it down the line.

According to Atkinson and Shiffrin, if the information is rehearsed and you repeat it over and over inside of the brain, then it is going to be transferred more into the long-term storage of your memories. You already automatically do this when the memory is important enough, such as when a big event happens in your life, and you keep replaying the scene in your head.

But, if there is something else that comes up that is important to you and you want to translate it into the long-term memory, you would simply need to give it some more attention and repeat it in your head. It would have a better chance of staying there for the long term.

3. Long-term memory

When the information is stored in the short-term memory for a longer period of time, it is then going to be automatically moved over to storage in the long-term memory, making it something that you are able to remember for a very long time. Things that you hold onto as important, those that are tied to an emotion and things that you repeat often will be placed into the long-term memory.

Many times a traumatic experience, or other experiences that were able to impact your emotions, will be able to get put in the long-term memory without much work on your part. The emotions have a big impact on whether or not the memory is going to stay in the short-term memory and then disappear, or if they will be brought into the long-term memory so that you can remember them in the future.

The long-term memory can hold onto these memories for a long time. In fact, the amount of time that a memory can stay there is indefinite. Sometimes it lasts for a year, and sometimes it will last for a lifetime. You may always remember a tragic car accident that you were in. You may always remember the birth of your children or your wedding day. These are important memories, often attached to an emotion that could remain in your life until your brain starts to deteriorate. That is one of the cool things about working with the long-term memory. There isn't a timer going off in the brain that determines how long a memory can stay. It can technically stay there forever.

Your Quick Start Action Step:

For this quick start action step, think back on a memory that you have held onto for many years. This one is stored in your long term memory. What are some of the reasons that you think it stuck in the long-term memory rather than the short-term memory? Why do you think you remember it all this time later rather than it fading away? Write down what you think.

Chapter 3: Powerful Photographic Memory Techniques Explained

Chapter 3: How to Prepare Your Mind for Photographic Memory Mastery

3.1

The first thing that we need to take a look at is how to prepare your mind to be able to master this new skill. It is going to take some time, and you may run into some challenges along the way. If you are not ready to run into roadblocks, then you may have even more trouble when it comes to this new skill. But if you learn how to work with your strengths and weaknesses, you will find that gaining a photographic memory is a great experience.

The human brain is designed so that it can gather information during every second of each day we are alive. Even when we are sitting here now and reading this book, the brain is concentrating on collecting and analyzing different information. You are focusing on the content that is in front of you. But the brain is making sure that you breathe, that your heart keeps beating, what the temperature is around you, how comfortable you are in the chair, and so much more.

The brain is able to store up more information that can be measured. It's true that the brain is only going to hold onto the information that it thinks is the most useful. That is why you are able to remember where the grocery store is located, even if you haven't been there for a few weeks. But, it is likely that you have forgotten the answers to a history test that you took back in high school.

As you keep going through the day, the brain is going to automatically work on filtering out all the information that it encounters. It is then going to store the information that it thinks is the most important, and then it will discard all the rest.

When you work with developing a photographic memory, you are starting to put yourself in control of the memories that you will store, and which ones the brain will forget. Basically, you are learning how to be proactive with your thought patterns, rather than just being a passive bystander. You will start to be an active part of all the moments in your life so that you can remember them better than before.

3.2

It is important that you prepare yourself for mastering your photographic memory. This is a tough process and the way that our modern world works results in us not being aware of the world around us. When you use some of the techniques that we talk about in the next session to help prepare your mind, you make the process so much easier. Simply learning how to be more observant about the world around you, and paying more attention and focusing, you will be able to really see improvements in your photographic memory.

3.3

Preparing your mind to get started with photographic memory does not have to be difficult. Some of the steps that you can do include:

1. Test yourself ahead of time

The first thing that you can do to prepare yourself for this process is to test yourself to see where your brain and memory is from the start. We talked about some examples of what you can do to test yourself, but this is a great starting point. Most of us have no idea where we stand when it comes to our memory. Many times we think that our memory is better than it is. Other times we may struggle in one area and do better in another.

When you take one of the tests to see how your memory is when you start, you are making it easier to see what you need to work on. Some people even go online and try out a few different tests so that they get the best idea possible of where their memories are right now before they even start. You may be surprised to find that your memory is not so good, and you need to start out at the beginning. It can also help you to have some realistic expectations and goals as you go through this process.

The tests are not meant to scare you. Yes, it's possible that you may get a bad score at some point, but this is at least a good gauge of where you are compared to where you would like to be. It doesn't mean that something is wrong with you if you don't start out where you would like to be. It just means that you need to adjust your goals and adjust the way you do things. Knowing this from the start can make it easier and will ensure that you progress better than if you just jump right in.

2. Putting down the electronic devices

Any time that you are practicing your photographic memory, those electronic devices need to be put away. You can occasionally use them if you want to test how far you have gotten with your practice, but it is often better to go with the workbooks and textbooks for this to help.

Electronics are designed to take your focus away. They don't require a whole lot of attention with them, and they can divert you from the task at hand. They are often going to impede your progress with the steps that we talk about in this guidebook. At least for the time that you are doing your exercises, turn off all the electronics and put them somewhere that you won't be tempted to use them. You will be amazed at what a difference it can make in your personal progress with remembering details.

If you feel brave enough, consider cutting down the amount of time you use electronics during all parts of your day. Too many of us miss out on things in life because we have our noses in the phones. And all we are doing is missing out on life because we want to see the latest update from a friend. And none of it really matters. If you really want to start seeing more progress with your photographic memory, then consider only using your electronic devices for an hour or two a day and then turning them off for the rest of the time. It will make a huge difference.

3. Try meditation

As we mentioned a bit above, one of the best things that you can do for yourself is add in some meditation to the day. These sessions don't have to be very long. Many have reported that just spending ten to twenty minutes a day in meditation and clearing their heads can make a big difference. And you can fit the session into whatever time works the best for you. Some people like to do it in the morning before they get up, some like to do it at night so they can sleep better, or you can even split it up into two short sessions to hit both these times.

There are different methods that you can use when it comes to meditation, and you can pick the one that is right for you. But if you would like to keep it simple and easy, these are some of the steps that you can try out to get started with meditation:

- Find a quiet place to go. It is really hard to meditate properly if you are in some place noisy or have the kids bouncing all around. It is best to find a suitable place that is quiet and where you can be alone while you do this. Have someone watch the kids and go into a quiet bedroom. It's only a few minutes of your day so make sure to schedule it off and be somewhere that no one can bother you.

- Get comfortable. Before you can do meditation, you need to be comfortable. The best way to do this is to sit on the floor with your legs crossed, your arms on your lap, and the back straight for easy breathing. You can add a pillow underneath you if this makes you more comfortable. For those that can't sit on the floor, you can use a chair. Just make sure that you have a straight back, your posture is good, and your feet are flat on the floor.

- Try to keep your mind clear. The point of meditation is to clear out your mind so that you can stop worrying about everything and start focusing on what is the most important. Focus on your breathing, letting it come in and out nice and deep. Try to push all those other thoughts out for the next ten to twenty minutes, and just focus on being at peace with yourself. This can be hard in the beginning, but if you keep trying and you are gentle with yourself, it is something you will achieve in no time.
- Try some music. Some people get started with meditation and find that it is impossible to keep their minds clear. They hear people walking around, the wind rustling

outside, the kids bouncing around, or even the air conditioner making a lot of noise. If you just can't get your mind to concentrate on the breathing, it may be time to add in a little music. This can help to calm you down and will clear out some of that other noise. Go with something nice and soft, like nature sounds, or classical music, for the best results.

- Use a word if you need. Keeping your mind clear can be tough. Some people find that repeating a word in their heads can make a difference. This can be any word that you want, as long as you are able to focus on that and nothing else. Go with something positive or uplifting for the best results.

- Set a timer. One thing that you can try, especially if you have a time limit for your session before you have to head to work or other obligations, is to set a timer at the beginning of your session. This keeps you from thinking about the time and always eyeing your watch or the clock. Set that timer and ignore the time until you hear it beeping. This really makes it easier for you to concentrate on the task at hand and can help you receive the benefits you want from meditation, while still making it to your other obligations on time.
- Keep the judgment away. In the beginning, you will find that it is really hard to keep your thoughts clear and on the task at hand.

Thoughts will always sneak in, such as important reminders, wondering what you need to get done for the day, and more. As you practice meditation, you will get better, and it will be easier to keep your thoughts and mind clear. But when those pesky thoughts do come in, don't be so hard on yourself. This happens to everyone. If you start feeling bad because these thoughts are there, you will just ruin the whole session as more and more thoughts rush in. Instead, when a thought finds you, just gently push it aside and continue on with your session.

4. Set some goals

A good way to prepare for getting started with this process is to set up some goals for you. You need to be able to set aside a good amount of time each day to work on your photographic memory. You don't need to spend hours upon hours doing this, but a good hour a day can make a big difference in your results.

Setting goals will give you an idea of what you need to work on and how much you can fit into your practicing time. An hour is a good amount of time for most people, so set a goal to help you spend that hour wisely. Maybe you will set a goal for how much you are able to improve in a week. Or you can say that your next goal is to be able to go to a party and remember the name of at least three people later on.

Your goals can be anything that you would like. The important part is that they motivate you and that they are challenging enough that you will have to put in some work to reach them. Some people want to get started on this process without goals, but writing down those goals and holding yourself to them (as long as they are realistic), can do wonders when it comes to how far you will go with your photographic memory.

Setting goals is one of the best ways that you can ensure that you are going to get the photographic memory that you want. Without these goals, you lose out on some great motivation that can keep you moving forward. Plus, you will have no idea how well you are doing or whether or not you are progressing, if you do not set some goals.

The goals do not have to be that complicated, and you can make them be whatever you would like. Some people decide what they would like to concentrate on first. If you are really bad with names of people you meet, you may want to set your first goal to learn how to remember names. If you are pretty good with the names, but can't remember a number to save your life, this can be your first goal.

Write down the goals that you want to

accomplish and then separate them down into actionable steps. If you want, you can even list out the deadlines for them. This helps you to keep moving forward, will hold you responsible for the work, and can show you how far you have come as you work through this whole process.

5. Realize that this can take some time

The whole process of working on your photographic memory can take some time. It is not something that is done overnight. You will not be able to wake up one morning and remember everything around you. And an important part of preparing your mind for doing well with all the techniques that we will talk about is realizing this.

Some people are determined that they must have a photographic memory overnight. They set themselves up with high expectations that things must work a certain way and that they must be really good at this. But all this is doing is setting you up for failure. Everyone learns at a different pace, and while some people may be able to fly right through these steps, others will need some more time.

Before you get started with any of the techniques in this guidebook, you need to understand that this process takes time and that you will need to work at it. It is fine to set up some challenges for yourself if you need them, but maybe try some of the techniques first and see how long you think they will take. All your goals need to be challenging for you, but still attainable and practicing with some of the techniques can make it easier to know where you stand and where you want to go.

If you start this out with realistic expectations, you will find that it is much easier to keep on with it and you won't get discouraged when the results are not instant. You will see success, and you will see improvements if you keep on working hard. But, you need to realize that it does take time.

Your Quick Start Action Step:

Your quick start action step is to find a few memory testing games to try out. You can choose to work with ones online or go with some in workbooks. You only need to spend a few minutes with each one so go ahead and try out a few. Write down the results so that you can check them out later on and see how much you improve.

Chapter 4: How to Achieve Photographic Memory

Chapter 4: Powerful Memorization Techniques

4.1

In some cases, you will be able to use various techniques to help you bring names, details, and numbers to your mind. This guidebook will talk about a few different options such as visualization, association, and more. But this does not work for all the things that you need to remember. In these instances, you will need to rely on memorization to help you to get these things in your memory. Memorization may not be as much fun as some of the other options, but it is a quick and effective way to see the results that you want.

During the ancient times, people did not have instant memorization aids to help them out. Writing out a long script would take up a lot of ink that was expensive, so they had to memorize the book or poem or other thing. Cue cards were not something that most of them would use. There were also no PowerPoints, visual aids, or other materials that could make it easier for them to remember information. This is why they often relied on memorization, and this technique is one that is all about pure skill.

To help them remember a lot of information, people would use several different techniques to help their brain hold onto many sets of data without needing to use aiding materials. These people were called mnemonists, which is a term that is used for those who possess an exceptional ability to recall many details with ease.

Since that time, these techniques have been shown to provide the user with some dramatic results, and many of them are still in use today. While they do require a lot of memorization, which no one really likes to do, they are a great way to help you start remembering the important facts that you want. Let's take a look at some of the different memorization techniques that you can use to make your photographic memory do better.

4.2

Memorizaiton techniques are going to be so important at making your life easier during this process. You are not going to be able to just look at something and remember it forever. You need to have some methods in place that can help you to get this done. The memorization techniques that we will talk about below will make this process much easier.

4.3

There are many different techniques that you can use to help you work on your photographic memory. Some of the most common options include the following:

1. **Rote Learning**

    a. Rote learning is one of the easiest methods to explain when it comes to memorization techniques, but it is the one that most people do not want to use to retain information. With this one, you will repeat lists of information many times until you can hold onto it in your memory. This method is not popular because it does not really require any kind of learning process and there isn't any creativity found in it.

b. Unless you spend more time than usual rehearing that information, the encoding process using rote learning is not going to last very long. In fact, it could start fading in just a few hours. This is why it is a good method for those who are trying to memorize lessons or cram for a big exam when they are short on time. You would have to spend a lot of time with rote learning to retain the information in the long-term memory.

2. Mnemonics

a. Another method that you can use, and which many students are going to rely on, is the mnemonic. This is used to help you memorize details that go together in a common list or group. Rather than spending the time memorizing the whole list, certain parts of the words or the initials will be combined to form another word, phrase, or sentence. This usually makes it easier to remember the information because you just need to remember the word or phrase that you picked out.

b. My very educated mother just served us nine pies is an example. This helps list out the planets in order and is easier to remember than Mercury, Venus, Earth, Mars, Jupiter, Saturn, Uranus, Neptune, and Pluto. You can make up any mnemonic device that you would like based on the information that you are trying to remember. There are a lot of these mnemonic devices out there that you can choose from, or get creative and see what you can come up with.

3. **Linking**

   a. When you use mnemonics and rote learning, you probably won't need to work with visualization to make them happen. But linking, along with all of the other techniques that we will talk about, will need to use visualization to help. Linking is a method that you can use to help connect adjacent details on a list. It is a way to visualize mental images that represent the connection of the first detail over to the second one, and then the second detail over to the third one, and so on until all the details are connected. Let's take a look at how you would be able to do this by first looking at the list of countries below:

United States
Canada
Bermuda
Iceland
Denmark
Switzerland
Ireland

San Marino

Norway

Luxembourg

b. Now, to use the linking method, you will need to come up with a visual for each of the countries that are listed. You may want to start out with some scenarios that have a picture of yourself, watching shooting stars (which can stand for the American flag), in slow motion. Then you can imagine that the stars hit the ground before transforming into maple leaves (like the leaves from Canada). Then, the maple leaves can start to turn green as they create a field of Bermuda grass (Bermuda). Then the Bermuda grass field will start to turn into an ice field (Iceland) as it gets cold.

c. And then, you would keep on with the visual from there. Again, make sure to exaggerate the scenarios and make them as outlandish as possible so that it is more likely our brain will be able to remember them. With this exercise, the visuals don't need to be realistic at all, as long as they link up with the words that you need to remember and they are something that stays in your memory.

4. Emotion-based memorization

   a. One of the most effective methods that you can use to help you do better with memorization is to add your emotions to it. The emotions are really strong, and they can help take otherwise ordinary information and memories and turn it into something that is stored in your long-term memory. You can also use your emotions as a technique to remember the important information later on.

b. With this technique, you are going to apply an emotion to each piece of information that is on your list. The emotion that you should associate with each detail should, as much as you can, be as distinct from the others as possible. You will need to have a pretty deep imagination since the emotions that come up during this visualization technique need to be felt by you as if they were real. If you just say the emotion without feeling it at all, then it is not really going to work for storing memories or information.

Your Quick Start Action Step:

Each of the options above can serve their purpose for helping you remember important things. Which one do you think will do the best for helping you learn things quickly that you don't need to remember very long? Which one do you think will help you to remember things in the long term?

Chapter 5:
The Importance of Visualization

Chapter 5: The Importance of Visualization

5.1

One method that you can try out when working on your photographic memory is visualization. This is basically a process of using your own imagination to help you remember the important details. You can definitely use this to your advantage when it comes to working on your own photographic memory.

To get started, there is one important rule to remember when you work with visualization. And that is to exaggerate everything. The more that you are able to exaggerate things in your mind, the easier it will become to recall them later on if you need them. Let's take a look at a few examples of how you can use visualization for your needs.

Let's start with Cupid, the tiger. Cupid usually doesn't have any kind of connection with an animal tiger. This means that you are going to have to create a visual inside of your head so that you will be able to remember that the tiger's name is Cupid. This is where you can exaggerate a little bit to help you remember. You could imagine a tiger who has pink fur, rather than the stripes, and one that has spots that are in the shape of small red hearts. Imagine that this tiger flies around the park with some wings on its back. This helped to combine the Cupid with the tiger and gave you a nice visual to look at so you can remember their name.

That is just one example of what you can do to use visualization. The next is Red, the elephant. Sure, the name red seems like it is easy, but if you are meeting a lot of different animals during the day, are you going to be able to easily remember it when the names mix together?

One way that you can attach the word red to the elephant is to maybe think of a red colored elephant that is as small as an ant. While elephants are never the size of an ant, it is an exaggeration that makes it easier for the mind to remember the color and the name of that particular elephant.

You can make any type of visualization

that you want for these names, but always remember to exaggerate it to better ensure that the mind will remember it later on. If your mind is able to enlarge something to be as big as a planet, it is then able to reduce it to something very small as well.

How visualization will stick with your memory

We already know that the amount of attention that we give to something is going to decide whether it is going to be encoded in the brain or not. For example, if you go through the park and happen to glance up at a couple walking by, it is not likely that you will remember them even ten minutes later. But if you keep walking and run across a cosplayer, you probably gave their outfit and the way they were acting a second look. You may not store this information in your long-term memory, but it's likely that you would remember it long enough to tell someone what you saw later on.

Things that are uncommon are going to cause you to pay more attention. So when the body senses that there is something strange going on, then the stimuli will automatically pass through the encoding stage, simply because you are paying more attention to it. And because you give it that extra attention for being unusual, it is going to enter into the storage process. How far it gets, or if it enters long-term memory, will depend on how unusual or how big of an impact it made on you.

The same thing is going to happen when

the brain works to create a mental image all on its own. Visualization of a scenario that happens on a day-to-day basis, such as taking a bath or eating, is not necessarily going to be held in your mind. These things don't require a lot of your attention, so you won't have them get stored in your long-term memory.

5.2

Many people are visual learners. Put a book in front of them and they may not be able to remember any of the information. But let them watch that same information in a movie, and they will remember it forever. Visualization can help these kinds of learners so that they can hold onto any information they learn along thew way.

5.3

For visualization to work, you need to add some exaggeration to the whole thing, or at least do something that is a little bit unique. Rather than just seeing an image of you eating a sandwich, you could imagine that you are eating a piece of chocolate cake that is as big as your house. Or think about the fact that you are sleeping in a bed that is able to float off on its own. When you think of these unusual situations, it is going to force the brain to pay more attention so that it can encode the stimuli.

When mental images are exaggerated and unrealistic, they have a better chance of sticking in your memory simply because the thing that makes them odd makes them easier to remember. When you retrieve out the memory, your brain is going to ready all of the available pictures that are there to help satisfy the thing that you want to remember.

However, we see a lot of images throughout the day, and sometimes there will be quite a few pictures in the brain that will look similar to the thing that you want to remember. This can result in a distorted or altered memory. And this can even cause some of your memories to overlap if you are not careful. But when something odd is encoded inside the brain, this means that there isn't other material there that can compare and cause conflict during retrieval.

So, when most people try to bring up a memory, it can get lost or confused because there are so many similar images inside their brains. But when they start to come up with an odd picture or one that is strange to help with a particular memory, there won't be something similar in the brain, so it makes it easier to remember. You can use this trick with almost anything that you would like to remember, you just need to make sure that your visual is as strange or unusual as possible.

Visualization is a tool that a lot of people like to work with. They like that it is pretty simple for them to use, and it is better than spending all your time just repeating the information and hoping that it sticks around. It does take some time to master, though. You need to learn how to find pictures that not only will be easy to think about later, but also ones that actually go with the thing that you want to remember. But with some practice, you will be able to get visualization to work well with you.

Visualization does not have to be hard. Some of the steps that you can follow to make this happen includes:

1. Get the picture in your head. You can do this with anything, just get a picture in your head.
2. Try to find ways to overexaggerate it. If it's a person with red hair, think that their hair is on fire. If it's a piece of food, imagine that it has legs and can walk around.

3. Any item, no matter how ordinary, can be used in visualization. While uncommon things are easier to remember, you can take a common item and make it uncommon in your mind.

Your Quick Start Action Step:

Go on a walk outside. Find something to focus your attention on. It can be something at the park, a bird flying overhead, someone who passes you. Just pick something. Now, close your eyes and try to overexaggerate it as much as possible. Practice this with different items until you are good at using visualization.

Chapter 6:
Can My Emotions Make a Difference?

Chapter 6: Can My Emotions Make a Difference?

6.1

Think back through some of the memories that you have from your past. Which ones stick out the most for you? Are you able to remember the first lesson that you had in high school? Or do you remember your first heartbreak? While it is unlikely that you remember the first thing that you learned in high school, or even most of the classes that you took in high school, everyone will remember their first love, no matter how fulfilling, sad, or painful it may be.

The fact that your first heartbreak was fulfilling, saddening or painful is the main reason that you still remember it no matter how many years have gone by. Information that has enough emotion behind it is the most likely to be encoded by the brain and then stored. As we mentioned earlier, emotions are going to play a large role in the encoding phase simply for the fact that your level of attention towards that stimuli will be very high. This means that emotions are pretty much a guarantee that you will have the information around that emotion encoded and it will get stored permanently in the brain.

Emotions also have the power to dominate the importance of information. The long-term memory is going to contain more memories that were driven by memories compared to those that you consciously injected into there. If you are asked to remember any happy moment, then it is likely that at least one is going to pop up in your head instantly. But if you are asked to recite your school's phone number, it is very unlikely that you can.

While it may help you out more to remember the phone number of your school, your brain is able to retrieve the happy moment easier because it is charged with feelings, in this case, of happiness. The phone number will need to be rehearsed many times before it stands a chance, no matter how important it is to you.

6.2

Our mind makes associations between what is important and what we get emotional about. The more emotional we are about something, the more likely it is to stick in our minds. That is why we can remember our high school graduation, but we can't remember what we had for lunch last week. Learning how to tie the emotions into your memories will help you to automatically store the situations and information that you want without quite as much work.

6.3

Your emotions are going to have a huge impact on how much you are able to remember when it comes to working on your photographic memory. Let's take a look at how this works:

The importance of mood

One emotional aspect that can be related closely to how well the memory functions is the mood. It is a less specific emotional state that is brought on not necessarily by external stimuli, but sometimes by other internal factors. The surroundings and the external events, which are going to be considered external factors, can also influence a mood, although the mood itself will be determined by your state of mind.

Mood is able to affect your memory in one to two ways. These two ways include mood dependence and mood congruence. Mood congruence is going to happen when you remember memories that are similar to the mood that you feel right now. So, when you are in a bad or irritable mood, there is a high possibility that it is easier for you to remember an event or memory in the past when you were also very irritated about something.

On the other hand, mood dependence is going to affect both the encoding and the retrieval phases. It suggests that recalling the event is going to be easier when it is encoded in the same mood that you currently have during retrieval. A good example of this is when some sort of information from the past is encoded in the brain while you are feeling happy. You will then find that it is easier for you to remember the situation if you feel happy when you retrieve it.

This doesn't mean that you wouldn't still be able to retrieve that memory without feeling happy, but it is going to be a lot more difficult. A happy memory being brought out when you feel miserable or sad or angry can be really hard. But if you are already happy, it is really easy to retrieve that memory.

Applying emotions to visuals

Now the problem with this is that not

everything you need to remember is going to have an emotion attached to it right from the start. You may need to study some information from the test, but it's unlikely that you have any emotional attachment to math equations. That is why; you need to apply your emotions to some of the visuals that you want to use. This can make it easier for you to hold onto those memories for as long as you need them.

Think about how you feel after fingernails scrape against the chalkboard. It probably gives you a shiver and makes you feel uncomfortable. This is an example of feeling illusory emotions, and it is a skill that you will need to enhance your retention with visualization. Also, when you are applying emotions here, you must remember that honesty is important. Focus on a feeling that is realistic to what you would get if the same thoughts happened in the real world.

Let's take a look at how this is done.

1. We will work with Bryce, the ostrich.
2. When he sees other birds that can fly, he starts to cry because he can't do the same thing.
3. Imagine here that you were born as Bryce. You are super excited about your future because you believe that the moment you grow up, you will also be able to fly.
4. But as you get older, you start to realize that you are not a bird

who can fly. You must live your whole life on the same ground without being able to witness how beautiful Earth is from above.

As you went through that situation, how did you feel? Did you feel sympathetic, frustrated, down? If what you felt was similar to one of those emotions, it means that you were able to project a realistic emotion out of nothing but a thought. If you did this effectively and concentrated on it hard enough, you may start to just see Bryce every time that you start to feel sad.

The biggest challenge here is that you need to be able to combine the fanciful and exaggerated pictures with some real and genuine emotions. This can be hard depending on the information that you want to put with it. But remember, there are quite a few emotions that you are able to work with. Go back to that math equation that you want to memorize. An emotion like frustration can work to help you remember it a little bit better.

Your Quick Start Action Step:

Practice tying in your emotions to the things that you see around you, or even to the things that you want to remember. If you are bad at remembering to grab your keys, consider tying an emotion to it when you set the keys down. Tie in anger at being late at work, joy for being able to go and pick up your kids, or maybe even fun for the great adventure that you had last summer in that car. You will find that when you can tie a strong emotion to the keys (or any other object), it is much easier to remember them.

Chapter 7:
How to Remember People's Names

Chapter 7: How to Remember People's Names

7.1

Now it is time to put some of the stuff we have talked about to work. This chapter is going to concentrate more on how you will remember the people you meet. Each day, we encounter many different people. Whether we see them on the street, have a friend introduce us to someone new, meet a new coworker, or go to a party and meet someone, it is important in our society to remember those people.

Forgetting the people we meet may be

pretty commonplace, but it can result in some embarrassments in the process. The other person may remember you, but you could be sitting there worried that you can't remember their name at all. With the techniques that we are going to discuss in this chapter, you will finally be able to remember the name, as well as other important details, about someone you meet, so you will never be in an uncomfortable position when encountering them again.

A big reason that your brain is going to have such a hard time remembering names is that during this process, there are so many different parts of the brain that are working at the same time. Not only does the brain need to recollect the name of the person, but it is working on facial recognition as well. When you meet someone in the past, your brain is responsible for storing the image in the part that is called the fusiform gyrus. This is the part that is located in the center of the right brain.

Then when it comes to memory, it is going to be stored in the hippocampus. The hippocampus is the medial temporal lobe of your brain. So, when you see someone you recognize, your brain is basically going into hyperdrive because it is doing several jobs at once. It will first try to remember where you saw that face for the first time, and since many faces are so similar, the brain is working really hard to match the face to the place. It then needs to remember the name from all that as well.

The good news is that with some

practice, your brain will not only be able to perform this kind of recognition easily and quickly, but it will be able to match a name to the face, without a big pause and a lot of trouble in the process. But how do you practice this?

7.2

There are many times throughout our lives where we will meet new people and will need to remember their names. If we are not able to do so properly, or we constantly forget names, it could be embarrassing and could even cause issues with our professional lives. Being able to learn how to remember the names of those we meet can make a big difference in how we react and interact with others at big social events.

7.3

The best way to practice this is through a method that is known as association. Studies have shown that any time the brain associates one detail with another detail; it will be able to better recall that detail. So, if the brain is able to associate a name with a mutual connection or a place, it is going to have a better chance of recalling the detail.

So, the easiest way to make sure that you are able to remember the name of someone you meet is through association. The thing that you choose to associate the name with is not going to be as important, each person is different. The biggest thing is that you need to be able to draw out that associate quickly so that you can remember the name the next time that you see them.

Let's look at this example. You head over to a family reunion. Your brother comes over to talk to you with his new girlfriend. This is going to be the first time that you meet her. Your brother introduces her as Angie. While you talk with your brother and his new girlfriend, you learn that she does work as a real estate agent. One way that you can choose to associate the name with the person is doing an association with her job. So, you may want to use something like Angie, the Agent.

This may seem like such a simple thing to work with, but it can actually do some wonders for helping you remember the people you meet. You need to do this right away to make it stick. In addition, when you first meet someone new, it is a good idea to say their name out loud. Doing this simple exercise is a great way to help the brain hear the information and then store it away for later use. So, when your brother first introduces you to his new girlfriend, you could repeat something like:

"Hello, Angie! It's so good to

meet you."

You can then take some time to say the name once more, maybe at the end of the conversation. The more that you can say the name out loud, without sounding strange, the easier it is for your brain to remember the name with the face later on. So, at the end of the conversation, you can consider saying the name again to help solidify the name of the person in your brain. Consider saying something like:

"Thanks so much, Angie! I hope we get the chance to talk again soon."

This is a very simple process to do, but association is an excellent way for you to start remembering the names of the people you meet. However, there are times when association may not be quite enough, and you will need to keep repeating the name to get it stored in the brain. If repeating the name one or two times doesn't seem to be doing the trick, you would just need to repeat the name through your mind as you start the conversation.

This can be pretty simple. As you start to talk to the person, you can say something like "Please, tell me about yourself." This will get the other person to stop talking, even for a few seconds, as they think of an answer, and then it gives you a few seconds of silence so that you can repeat their name through your head a few times to get it to stick.

Now, as you work on this process, you will actually be amazed at how little you need to pay attention to a conversation to hear what the other person is saying. If saying the name a few times is not enough for you, then you need to practice repeating the name through your mind while the other person talks. You can say it a few times in between listening to the story the other person is sharing, and it won't make you miss out on anything. Then, when it is your turn to start sharing and talking, you have a great start on knowing and memorizing what the other person's name is.

When it comes to association, perfection is not that important in the beginning. Sure, you want to get to the place where you are able to remember names when you run into a new person later on, but right now, you need to focus on forming new habits.

Instead of spending your time stressed out or worried that you must get it right the first time that you practice on association, it is much better to focus on the method itself. This will help you to learn the names of everyone you meet, and over time, the association method will be your go-to method to ensure you can remember a name, no matter what. The good news is, you can repeat the name in your head as often as you want because no one is able to read your thoughts. This can take some of the pressure off, and you can have some freedom when working through each step.

Before we move on, there are a few important things that you should remember to help you do well with the association method and to ensure you are able to actually start remembering the names of those you meet. The steps to help you include:

1. Repeat the name out loud when you first say hello to the other person.
2. See if you are able to find some association between the name and a detail about the person that you can remember. When you use the association Angie the Agent, it helps you not only remember her name but also helps you remember what she does for work.
3. Repeat the name in your head over and over again. If the conversation is longer, you will then have plenty of time to get it

down and start to remember it. Even with a shorter conversation, this gives you ample time to repeat the name.

4. When it is time to say goodbye to this person, make sure to say the name out loud again. This helps solidify it in your brain and will make it easier to remember later.

Your Quick Start Action Step:

Go to your local coffee shop or to the library. The location doesn't matter as long as you meet someone new there. Introduce yourself and start up a conversation.

Use the steps above to help you

remember the name and see how long you can keep that name in your head.

Chapter 8: The Steps You Need to Memorize Numbers

1 2 3 4 5
6 7 8 9 0
+ × ÷ −

Chapter 8: The Steps You Need to Memorize Numbers

8.1

Many people would be just happy being able to use the association rules that we talked about in the last chapter to remember names. They have found themselves in many situations where they run into people they have met and can't remember the name. Sometimes the other person understands, and other times it can lead to an embarrassing situation.

If you are working with gaining a photographic memory, we need to take it to the next level. This chapter is going to take some time to look at the steps that are needed to start memorizing numbers. There are many times when you will find that memorizing numbers within a few minutes of seeing them can be really useful.

You may need to memorize a license plate. You may need to get someone's phone number and have it ready for later. You may want to use it to remember an address, and there are a lot of times when your day can fill up with numbers. The problem here, though, is that numbers are one of the most difficult things to memorize, even for those who are working with a photographic memory.

As you work on developing your memory a bit through the steps in this guidebook, the easier it is for you to learn and memorize numbers quickly. However, since we are just getting started, you are going to have to spend some time with learning number memorization.

Number memorization can be a bit tricky, and it will take you more time to master than the association that we worked on in the last chapter. The good news is that achieving the ability to memorize all sorts of numbers is not impossible. And just like with other parts of the brain, finding a simple method to use is often going to be enough to help you remember any string of numbers that you come across during the day.

The main reason that memorizing

numbers is harder than remembering names is that when you are working with numbers, there is nothing there to associate them with. Angie the Agent is pretty easy to remember because you already know that she's a real estate agent and they work well together. This works with a lot of names and occupations that the other person may have. But when you have a larger number, how are you going to associate the numbers with something to help you remember.

Even visualization can be hard here. If you sat down and thought about a dog, it wouldn't take long for a picture to come up with some type of dog. But if you were asked to visualize the number 12843432, the odds are that it would be really hard for you to do without the right techniques in place.

8.2

Memorizing numbers is a great way to help you get ahead. If you are in accounting, you may need to remember numbers to get your job done. You may need to remember a number to know the balance of your bank account. You may need to know a number in order to get your destination. There are so many times when you will need to know a number and writing it down can be a hassle and even unsafe.

8.3

While association with numbers is difficult sometimes, there are still association methods that you can work that can make it easier. You will not be able to use a direct association method like we did with Angie, the Agent, but you can create your own alternate associations that go with each number. Then, you can use that step to fill in some of the details that you need in your mind.

To get started with this, we first need to learn how to associate the numbers that you want to remember with details. We are going to do this by assigning a number to a specific object.

There are a few methods that you can do to make this happen. One method that many people will choose is to associate each number with a letter of the alphabet. It would look something like the following:

    1 = A
    2 = B
    3 = C
    4 = D
    5 = E
    6 = F
    7 = G
    8 = H
    9 = I
    0 = J

You would then take some time to memorize this list until you are able to match each number to the letter that it corresponds to. The more you practice this list, the faster you will be able to match the parts together.

This may seem confusing right now, so let's take a look at an example of how this would work. You are given the number 14,625 that you need to memorize. Going off the list that we used above, you would end up with the letters ADFBE. This may not make a lot of sense now, but if you used those letters to create an acronym, it could work better. You may use something like All Ducks Fly Back East. Now you have a nice visual that you can use in your mind to help remember the numbers with. You can always change the acronym that you use, that was just a way to help you get started.

That is not the only way that you can remember numbers. Another good method to use is to incorporate association to the numbers with some mind pictures. We are going to make a list again so that it assigns a detail or an item to the number. An example of this would be the following:

1 = Dog
2 = Cat
3 = Bird
4 = House
5 = Car
6 = Balloon
7 = Watch
8 = Apple
9 = Grass

10 = Umbrella

You would then go through and memorize this list again so that you are easily able to associate the object that you chose with the number within a few seconds of seeing the number. Remember that you are able to change up the objects or the details that go with the number. This is just one way to help you get started. Once you have this list memorized, you would then be able to see a string of numbers and use it to help you remember.

For this example, we are going to use the number 54,823. Going from the list that we used above, the details that go with it would be Car, House, Apple, Cat, and Bird. You can then change this into some visuals. You can imagine that you are driving your car in front of a house that has an apple tree in the front and there is a cat in the branches going after a bird.

Of course, this method is a little more complicated, but when you are able to visualize the picture that goes with the numbers, it is more effective than just reading the number and hoping that you remember it.

One thing to remember is that when you use these associations, you must put the items in the image in the exact same order as they appear in the number line. If you mix them up, then you are going to get the number mixed up. You need to do it in the right order, even if the image is harder to come up with, to ensure that you come up with the exact number that you are supposed to be memorizing later on.

As you can see, it is a bit harder for you to remember numbers than it is to remember names of people you just met. However, you are able to use both or either of these tricks to make it easier. And if you take some time memorizing the lists above, or making your own list that corresponds to each number, then it is going to be a lot easier. In fact, as you get better at memorizing those lists, you will find that it won't matter how long the number is, you will be able to remember it later on.

Just like with any of the methods that we practice in this guidebook, practice is going to make you better at it. You will not be able to start with this method today and see results tomorrow. But if you take the time to work on these lists and practice, and you learn how to focus on what you are doing, you will find that numbers, and the associations that we worked on in this chapter, will come as second nature to you and you will be able to do them in the future without even thinking that hard.

To summarize, there are several steps that you should take

1. Decide which method you would like to use. Some people like one that is simple, some need it to be more complicated.
2. If you are picking out words, make sure to memorize which ones you are using with each number.

3. Practice this for at least five to ten minutes each day. After a few weeks it will stick.
4. After you know the numbers and the words or letters they are associated with, practice. You can make up number or think of ones that are important to you, and then practice using your own system.

Your Quick Start Action Step:

The first exercise is to list out the numbers 0 to 9 and then give them a corresponding letter or word to help you remember them. Spend a little time memorizing this to make it easier to bring these to mind later on.

Chapter 9: It's All in the Details

Chapter 9: It's All in the Details

9.1

The techniques that we discussed in the previous chapters are great ways to ensure that you can increase your memory power and start to remember things better than ever before. But for any of them to work, you need to learn how to pay attention to details. It is way too easy to go through life and not pay attention to any of the details that are going on around you. This may seem like the easiest way to get through things but think of all the things that you are missing out on. And if you are not paying attention to the little details, there is no way that you will work on your photographic memory.

There are a lot of different reasons why it is so important to pay attention to the details. In fact, you will find that an impressive thing about having one of these photographic memories is that it allows you to have a higher ability to pay attention to these details. You will be able to pay attention to what is going on around you, and you will soon be able to recall even the most specific things from stuff that happened last week, last month, last year, or even long ago.

The biggest reason that most people have so much difficulties with recalling what went on with a particular experience is that they didn't pay attention to the details when it happened. You may be too focused on the phone in your hand, worrying about what happened in the past or will happen in the future, or something else may take up your attention. With all these other things going through your mind, you may miss out on what is happening right in front of you right now.

If you want to be able to work on your photographic memory, you must learn how to train yourself to pay attention to all the little things that are going on right in front of you. And you also need to train your mind to pick up on these things and then store them to make it easier to recall later.

9.2

The details are the most important part

when it comes to remembering things. If you just generalize it in your head, the mind will assume that this situation, person, place, or something else is not that important to you. The more details that you are able to put with that situation or thing, the easier it will be to keep it in your long-term memory to hold onto for the long term.

9.3

Steps on How to Remember Details Better:

1. The first thing that you must do to make this happen is to learn how to slow down. In our modern world, we spend a lot of time moving fast. We have access to a lot of information online, and we

want to access it now. We need to get a lot of stuff done for work, so we rush around. We are always online with social media, and we see things uploaded and changed all the time. Add in other obligations, school functions, keeping up with the kids, and more, and it is really hard to keep track of the details in this fast-paced world.

2. Instead of having your head in the phone or letting yourself get caught up in all the busyness that seems to follow you around, it is time to take a step back and really look at what is going on around you. Life is enjoyed when you start to look at the details that are going on around you. Sure, you

could rush through life, and you will be fine, but think of all the things that you are missing out that are right in front of you.

3. Try this experiment the next time that you are out. First, put down the phone because you are not going to do well with this if you have your nose in the phone. Take a look around you, no matter where you are. What is the person in front of you wearing? What is the name of the clerk who is helping you at the store? How does the air feel when you are outside? Do you smell anything in the air? What is the color of the car right in front of you?

a. These are such simple questions, but we are often so busy running around that we end up missing out on it and not actually paying attention to things and miss out on these details. You will be surprised at how much you are able to notice when you just take the time to ask questions and look around.

4. In addition to asking these questions so that you can slow down the mind and start focusing on this moment, you should also work to make a deliberate effort to be present in this moment. As you work on the mindfulness that

we talked about before, you will learn more of how to make this happen. While you are looking around and asking some of the questions from above, make sure that you keep your mind free and just think about what is going on. Do not worry about what will happen when you get to the office or what will happen in the future. Just learn how to empty out your mind and focus on what is going on in the here and now.

5. You may be wondering what this has to do with your photographic memory. Why would you want to spend so much time concentrating on being in the here and now, when you really want to get better at memorizing

what is going on around you? When you take the time to become more aware of the life that is around you, of the things that are going on around you, you will find that your brain is able to naturally pick up on more details. This is going to come in handy later on when you get into situations where you must make the effort to remember the details of something.

To really see success when it comes to training your brain to be good at photographic thinking, it is so important for you to take the time to engage all of your senses. The more senses you are able to engage in this process, the easier it will be to start remembering more. Yes, this does take a lot of conscious effort to make it happen. But the more work and effort that you put into the process, the easier it becomes, and it will even start to feel more natural in the future.

Your Quick Start Action Step:

Take the time to observe the things around you. Go out on a walk and really look at what is there. Notice how many flowers are out. Notice that the birds are singing around you. Notice that the sun is shining, what other animals are out, and more. You only have to be out for a few minutes to make this work, but make sure that you focus on what is going on around you as much as possible.

Chapter 10: Putting it Altogether – How to Achieve Photographic Memory Mastery

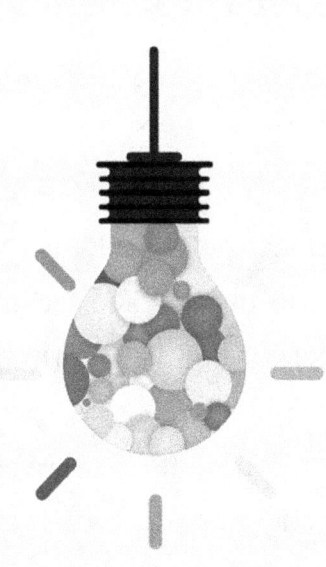

Chapter 10: Putting It Altogether – The Steps You Need to Achieve Photographic Memory

10.1

This guidebook took a lot of time to look at some of the tips and techniques that you can use to work on your photographic memory. These are good places to start to ensure that your memory is going to start remembering people, numbers, and even important details about your life. For some people, this is enough to help them get started on their journey of doing well with their photographic memory. All they need to do now is keep on practicing.

For others, it is helpful to have some more steps to make the process easier. In this chapter, we are going to take some time to break down the method that you need to do this, going step by step, in your own life. Let's take a look at the steps that you need to follow to make sure that you can increase your own photographic memory.

10.2

We spent a lot of time discussing the different things that you can do to help work on your photographic memory. There was a lot to take in. The action steps in this chapter are going to focus on what you need to do in order to put it all together so that you have an idea of what you need to do to make your memory as strong as ever.

10.3

1.

Take a look at your memory right now

Each person has a different type of memory. Some people think that they already have a pretty good memory, while others know that they can barely remember anything to save their lives. Before you can work on gaining a photographic memory though, you need to assess your skills and figure out where they are right now.

You can take a quick quiz or use another tool to help you assess where your memory is right now. You can do a simple online search for memory games or memory tests, and you will find a lot of valuable materials. These are pretty simple, such as looking at an image for a few seconds and then answering questions related to that image or you will watch a video before answering questions about the details. When you are done with the assessment, you will be given a score that will help you to see where your skills are in regards to memorization.

Don't take it badly if your score is not as good as you would wish. That is the point of working on your photographic memory. This gives you the chance to improve your memory, but you will never have an idea of whether you are doing well or not if you first don't know where to start. No matter how good your memory is, you will use the same skills and methods to help make the memory better.

2. Unplug those electronics and focus on the task at hand

Our modern world spends a lot of time on their electronics, checking emails and social media or just messing around without getting anything done. And no matter how hard it may seem to believe, you are not really going to miss out on anything if you turn off the electronics and spend some time focusing on your real life. Even if you focus on something as basic as putting gas in the car, you will soon learn that it can be much more interesting for your day than concentrating on what someone posted as their breakfast online.

Many of us have become brainwashed to think that we can only be connected to others and to the world if we spend all day long on our phones or other mobile devices. However, studies show that the more time you spend with your electronics, the less time you are engaging with the world around you and the less connected you really are to others.

By unplugging the electronics, at least while you work on your photographic memory, you are doing yourself a favor. You are giving yourself a chance to focus on your real life, and that will instantly make all the methods and techniques we talk about in this guidebook easier to do.

3. Spend at least an hour working on your memory

Just like with working out or spending time meditating each day, you can't expect to spend a few minutes on the memory each day and then see some big changes. You should commit some real time to this task if you want to actually see your photographic memory improve.

You would be surprised at how much your mind is able to wander, especially if you don't make a deliberate effort to keep yourself in the here and now. You need to work hard on this process and give it your all, for a good hour or more each day. This will make it easier for you to see results, and you will find that your photographic memory improves as well as your ability to focus on the here and now rather than worrying about things that already happened or will happen in the future.

4. Learn how to detox your mind

Although making a decision to only focus your attention on the current moment can be a constant effort, learning how to clear your mind of all that mental clutter that is in the way is not. Through some daily exercises, that can include both mental and physical exercises, you will be able to clear your mind of all the clutter and the garbage that your mind is holding onto, and that is eating up the energy that you should be using on your photographic memory.

The more clearly that you are able to look at the world around you, the easier it will be for you to capture as well as to store any details about situations you find yourself in. Mental junk, however, can build up in your mind quickly and often it finds its way there without you realizing it is there, or that it is actually pretty bad for you.

The best solution to this is to go through a mental detox. You simply go through the clutter that is in your mind and decide what is worth holding onto and what you need to get rid of. And if you decide to get rid of something, you learn how to let it go and not worry about it any longer.

5. Use intention to help advance your skills

When you are ready to learn anything new, it is going to take some deliberate effort. Changing your habits can be hard as well and will be a deliberate effort. Sharpening up the skills that you already possess will be a deliberate effort as well. You will need to put in all of your efforts to see changes when you do the photographic exercises that we discuss in this guidebook.

It is not enough to just hope that you are able to see some results when it comes to working on your photographic memory. This will take time and a lot of effort to make that change. Remember that some of your old habits are going to be hard to break. So, if you are truly looking to make a change in your life, then you need to make the deliberate effort to ensure that it happens, rather than just hoping that it will work for you.

Of course, when you do see some success in your skills, such as finally being able to remember names or seeing that you can remember a long string of numbers or other details in your life then go ahead and celebrate that small victory. It is a big deal, no matter how small, and celebrating it can help give you the motivation you need to keep working hard.

6. Take a look at your diet

The next step that you can try to improve is your diet. You will be amazed at how much your diet can affect your memory. There are certain substances, such as alcohol, that can have a big negative impact on your memory. But things like artificial sweeteners or sugar can have just as bad of an impact on the memory, and sometimes it can even be worse if the intake is pretty high.

All the parts that come with your body are designed to work together to keep you alive and functioning well. The body is almost like a machine. In that, it will run off whatever fuel you put inside of it. Of course, if you want it to work at its peak, you must make sure that you provide the body with the right kind of fuel.

If you put a lot of chemicals and junk food into the body, you are basically asking it to function without the right fuel. This is a foolish concept that doesn't make much sense, but one that a lot of people try to accomplish anyway. There are times when you can have some junk food as a treat, but if you really want to work on your photographic memory and see some results, then it may be time to try improving your diet.

7. Practice your photographic memory with some memory enhancing tools

In the first step, we took a look at some

games and tests that would give you a good idea of how good your memory was when you got started. But you can also use these games and tests in a way to sharpen and enhance your memory. And when you use them along with some of the other methods we discussed in this guidebook, you will be surprised at how much better your memory can become.

You can choose to do this with a computer if you would like. But there are also some great workbooks and paperback books that can do the same thing, and still, allow you to stay unplugged from the electronics. You can even do some matching games using cards to help make your memory a bit better.

8. Learn how to concentrate better

A lack of concentration is going to make it difficult for your mind to get things done. When you are not able to concentrate on the task at hand, it becomes almost impossible to get it done. You need to learn how to concentrate better if you want to also improve your memory as well as your work performance.

Yes, people are very skilled at being able to multitask during the day, but our brains are set up to only concentrate on one thing at a time. Trying to get more than that done at the same time can make life difficult. Sure, there are those people who seem to be really good at doing multiple things in a short amount of time. But this is not because they spend a lot of time learning how to multitask. It's because they have spent some time learning the art of concentration and it has worked out well for them.

These people are not spending a lot of time worrying about what occurs outside their workspace. They don't care about the company gossip. They keep their social media accounts, and emails turned off. And they often close their doors, so that they can get as much work done in a short amount of time as possible. You can use the same idea to help you out as well.

You can use the art of concentration no matter what you are doing. Whether you are trying to learn the different methods of photographic memory or you want to sue it to get more done at work, learning how to concentrate on the task at hand is a great way to improve your memory.

9. Learning how to focus

Focus and concentration are going to be two things that are tied together well, and many people are going to use these terms interchangeably. However, there are different degrees of concentration, but focus is a deliberate and undeterred effort to get something done.

While you are able to find some different degrees of concentration, there isn't a different degree when it comes to focusing. And when you figure out how to focus on something, you are telling your mind that this item is not trivial. When your brain takes the time to focus on something, it is basically giving all its concentration and attention and its efforts to this one thing. You can learn how to concentrate on something pretty quickly, but it does take a lot more effort to learn how to focus, and even more to learn how to implement that focus when you need it much.

As with all the other parts of photographic memory that we have talked about, you are able to turn your focus on, and you can also turn that focus off, just like with a light switch. You are the one who is in-charge of your own mind, which means that you are also in control when it is time to focus on something or not. When it comes to using your photographic memory, you can use this focus to your advantage to pay attention to the important details that you want to remember.

10. Never give up and never stop advancing

One major issue that comes up when you are working on developing your photographic memory is that as time goes by, your skills will start to fade away. This is not an issue of the photographic memory, but more of a result of how you are handling your memory.

You can't try out these techniques and do well with them, and then never practice again and hope that your skills are going to stay sharp and always be there when you need them. Just like with anything, your mind needs to be exercised all the time to stay strong. And the memory is not an exception to this.

As you go through the process of enhancing your photographic memory, you should never reach a point where you think that you are done. If you do reach this point, you are likely to stop working, and that means that all your skills will just slide backward.

Never stop developing the skills that you need for a photographic memory. There are always more things that you can practice, more things to observe in your daily life, and more ways that you can make the memory stronger. Never think that you have done enough and that it is time to stop, or all that hard work will just slip away.

Your Quick Start Action Step:

For this quick start action, you will need to come up with the plan for working on all the steps we've talked about in this guidebook. Bring out your calendar and decide how long you will work on your memory each day and what time. Schedule it in to make sure you don't forget. Then write out a list of the things that you want to work on, starting with the most important. Having a good plan in place will make all the difference when you get started so you can stay on track.

Bonus Chapter: How to Developer Laser Sharp Focus for Better Results

Bonus Chapter: How to Develop Laser Sharp Focus for Better Results

12.1

As we mentioned a bit earlier, developing your focus can make a big difference in the amount of things you are able to remember. Simply by focusing on something, you are telling the brain that this item or event is important. That can make it more likely that you will be able to encode and store that item or situation.

What this means for you is that, if you are able to learn how to focus better on the world around you, or at least on the things that you find important, you will be able to encode and store it better. This chapter is going to take some time to discuss how you can develop laser sharp focus so that you can see the best results possible.

12.2

Focus is so important when you get started with photographic memory. Your mind is more likely to store information that you focus your attention on. So, even if it ends up being a tiny little detail, if you put all your focus on it, your brain is going to assume that this detail is important. Here, we are going to take a look at the importance of focus on your memory and the steps that you can try to add in some more focus into your daily life.

12.3

Some ways to develop better focus:

1. Practice your meditation

We spent some time talking about

meditation earlier on, but practicing meditation is one of the best ways to ensure that you are able to keep your focus on the task at hand. With just one twenty-minute session, or two ten-minute sessions a day, you are going to notice in a short time how much your focus is able to improve.

2. Listen to music

A good way to help you get started with your photographic memory, especially if the information we are talking about seems really complicated, is to just listen to music. This doesn't mean just turn it on and let it play in the background. You need to really listen to what the music is saying.

As you start to listen to the music closely, you will notice a few things. You will not only realize what the artists are saying in their lyrics, but you can start to recognize the different instruments that are in the background. You will start to hear the individual notes, the changes in the beat, and so much more. And you will actually start to enjoy what is happening with the music more than just hearing it in the background.

Listening to music is a great way to focus your attention and get yourself back on track. It's a great way to give your brain a break from the task you are working on if you get bogged down. And, it can also help you learn how to focus your energy more when you get back to the task.

3. Cut down the goals to have immediate targets

You may have the goal of working on your photographic memory and being able to remember the details of your life better, but that is a pretty big goal without any specifics. You may not know what to specifically focus on, and that can make you have a lot of trouble.

With any goal that you decide to pursue, you need to break it up into more manageable pieces. When you list out exactly what you want to do, and give yourself smaller pieces to work on, it is easier to stay focused. You know exactly what you are supposed to be doing and when it should be done.

For example, you may have the goal of doing better with your photographic memory. The first goal would be working on learning names. You can make it a goal of the first party to remember the names of two new people. When you succeed at that, you can increase it to five people. And then keep increasing the number until you are able to remember the names of everyone at the gathering.

Then for your second goal, you can start to remember strings of numbers. Start with a shorter number, maybe four pieces in it. Then increase it to six, and then ten, and all the way up to twenty or more. You can also increase your goals of working on visualizing techniques and more. The goals you have and their timelines matter, but it's more important that you are able to give yourself clear-cut and short-term goals to keep your mind focused.

4. Work at the time that is most comfortable for you.

To help with your focus, you need to find the time that is best for you to get work done. Some people work best in the morning. Some people find that they do better later at night. And some work better in between these two times. You are never going to get your focus on point if you try to force yourself to work during a time that is not ideal for you. If you don't already know the time that works for you, then it is time to experiment and learn when you should be doing your work to be the most productive and focused.

5. Try doing some fasting

When you eat a heavy meal, it can slow you down and makes it harder to focus. This is because the body is directing the blood over to your stomach so that you can digest your food. The result is that you are sleepy, and you will have a hard time focusing on the task ahead. Fasting may be an option for you.

This does not mean that you need to spend weeks fasting and not eating a thing. That is not healthy for you and can make you sick and ruin your health. Plus, it won't do much for your focus. But, a small amount of fasting can have a lot of benefits. It can help to speed up your metabolism, and it can keep you alert. If you can't completely give up eating, you can consider a juice fast as well.

A good way to do this is to wake up in the morning and skip breakfast for an hour or two. During that time, you can focus on the work that needs to be done, whether it is a project for the office or working on the exercises we have in this guidebook. When you are done, you can go sit down and eat breakfast.

All you did here is move the eating time by a few hours at most. But the amount of work that you will be able to get done in that time period is amazing. You still get to eat, you will still take in the same amount of calories (unless you decide to turn this into a diet plan), but you will get so much done.

6. Make it a challenge, but not too much

If something is too easy for you, you can easily become bored with the whole process. You will give up because it seems too easy, and you don't see any progress in the process. Of course, if you make it too difficult, you will end up failing as well because you won't be able to complete the work, and you also won't see progress.

The point here is that you need to take some time to set up challenges, but be realistic. Know what your limits are in terms of how well your memory works, what your starting point is, and how much time you have to devote to this. Make sure that you are challenging yourself a bit, so that you have to work hard to see results, but don't make it so hard that you have no chance of success at all.

7. Delay your gratification

There have been some studies that show how delaying your gratification can make you more likely to succeed. There is some merit in this because when you delay your immediate gratification, you are able to focus more on the bigger picture rather than letting yourself get so distracted.

You can easily add this into your daily life. You can let someone else have the final piece of cake, even if you wanted it. Say no to the extra cheese on your sandwich. Finish cleaning up that room in the house before you get started on relaxing. It may be hard in the beginning because most of us are used to getting everything that we want right from the start. But after some practice, you will find that it's easier to say no to things, allowing you to say yes to the right things.

How does this help with focus? When you have to limit the amount of things that you are allowed to say yes to, you can delay gratification. This will help you to focus more on what's important to you, and you can use that focus to help you work on your photographic memory.

8. Spend some time outside

The best thing that you can do for your

focus is to spend some time with nature. We spend way too much of our time inside. Between work, cleaning the house, getting supper done, going to school, and the cold winter months, we can easily spend most of our time inside.

If you ever find that you are trying to accomplish something, whether it is finishing a project or working on the photographic memory exercises, and you just seem to be stuck, it may be time to take a break and go outside. Even half an hour outside, walking around and enjoying the fresh air and the sights can be enough to help you clear your head and regain your focus.

There are a lot of simple things that you can do to ensure you get your focus back when you spend time in nature. Go for a walk around the block. Find a park and smell the flowers. You can even just go sit in your backyard and take in the sounds and the fresh air. It doesn't have to be complicated. It just has to get you away from your work, so that you can give your brain a break and bring back the focus.

Many people have trouble convincing themselves to get up from the desk and go outside. They think that they will get more done sitting there. But if your focus is gone, you are going to waste your time and get nowhere. You will actually get further ahead if you take the time to enjoy some of nature for a bit, and then come back with a fresh mind.

9. Add in a bit of buffer time

Before you get started on something new, you should consider giving yourself a little buffer time. Too often, we run out of time during the day, so we end up cramming things together right on top of each other. But, it is so important to have a kind of a transition time between one task and the next one that we need to start.

Having that time to wind down rather than rushing into the next thing gently can make a big difference. First off, this allows us to have some breathing room to relax and get ready for the next thing. It also helps the brain to have a moment to switch gears. When you switch right away, the brain may be stuck on the last task, and you will just waste time trying to get started on something new. If you add in this buffer time, even five minutes, you will be able to regain your focus at the right times.

10. Get the little things out of the way

One of the things that can really get in the way of your focus is having a lot of little things that you need to get done, but you are procrastinating on. Rather than letting those things set and not get taken care of, you need to get them done. Sure, they may be a little unpleasant, but they usually don't take more than a few minutes to complete. Spend ten to twenty minutes working on these to get them done, and you will see that your mind all of a sudden frees up to focus on the things you need.

11. Exercise your body and mind each day

Keeping the mind and the body ready to go each day can make it so much easier to focus on the things around you. First, let's look at exercising your mind. There are tons of ways that you will be able to do this. Simply working on some of the exercises that we have in this guidebook each day can do wonders for working out that mind. You can also build up something creatively, talk to other people, do a crossword, or work on a puzzle.

The important thing here is not to let your mind get idle. When the mind gets idle, then it will start to have trouble focusing. It will let thoughts drift in, it will get distracted, and it will have a hard time doing what you want. When you work it out each day, enough that it feels strong but not all the time, so it gets worn out, you will see some great results.

Exercising the body is important as well. Without taking care of your body, you will feel sluggish, and your brain can go into kind of a fog. You do not have to go as far as being ripped, but your body is an asset in this process. Take a few minutes walk each day, clean the house, go dancing, or just do something that gets you up and moving.

Having laser-sharp focus is so important in helping you get the results that you want with your photographic memory. When you learn how to focus better, you will automatically be able to increase how much stuff you are able to remember. Follow these simple steps, and you are sure to see your focus increase in no time.

Your Quick Start Action Step:

Work on improving your focus. You can pick the method that works the best for you, but spend half an hour doing this. You can choose to listen to music and see if you can hear the different instruments. Consider doing some physical activity before your activities. Just make sure that you spend some time working on gaining better focus overall.

Conclusion

Thank you for making it through to the end of *Photographic Memory Mastery*. Let's hope it was informative and able to provide you with all of the tools you need to achieve your goals whatever they may be.

The next step is to try out the techniques that we discussed in this guidebook. Anyone is able to work on their photographic memory. It is not just something that only a few people are born with, and the rest of us have to stumble around and hope that we can remember things. Anyone can use the tips and tricks that are found in this guidebook to help you to slowly but surely work on your photographic memory.

When you are ready to start remembering things, such as important details, names of people, and even strings of numbers, make sure to take a look at this guidebook and learn all the techniques that you need to master your photographic memory.

www.ingramcontent.com/pod-product-compliance
Lightning Source LLC
Chambersburg PA
CBHW071238070526
44583CB00017B/2240